DOWN THE GAR___ ____
Privies in and around Bristol and Bath

by

LINDA HALL

COUNTRYSIDE BOOKS
NEWBURY • BERKSHIRE

First published 2001
© Linda Hall 2001

COUNTRYSIDE BOOKS
3 Catherine Road
Newbury, Berkshire

To view our complete range of books,
please visit us at
www.countrysidebooks.co.uk

ISBN 1 85306 700 8

Cover illustration by Louis Mackay
Produced through MRM Associates Ltd., Reading
Printed by Woolnough Bookbinding Ltd., Irthlingborough

CONTENTS

FOREWORD 5

1 A SHORT HISTORY OF LOOS 7

2 UP THE GARDEN PATH 23

3 RATS AND CREEPY CRAWLIES 31

4 ONE, TWO AND THREE HOLERS 35

5 'BUCKET AND CHUCKIT' 44

6 WHATEVER THE WEATHER 53

7 THE PLEASANT RETREAT 58

8 MISHAPS AND MISCHIEF 69

9 CHILDHOOD MEMORIES 78

10 THE PRIVY TODAY 85

ACKNOWLEDGEMENTS 93

ODE TO THE GARDEN PRIVY 95

The author inspects a single-holer at Mill Farm, Siston and its lid with two neat finger holes. This is now a garden shed. (Photo by Catherine Hall)

FOREWORD

What does the term 'privy' conjure up to most people? A small building at the bottom of the garden, a long trek on a winter's night, frightening spiders, a place for an uninterrupted read? All these and more, as the following pages will show. I have learnt to recognise the different types of privy at a glance, and can spot one over a garden wall without any hesitation. I hope that by the end of this book you will understand my enthusiasm!

When I was asked to write this book, I had spent many years recording the old farmhouses and farm buildings of South Gloucestershire, but I have to confess that I had rarely even noticed if there was an old privy amongst the other buildings, let alone taken any photographs. Yet the area is full of privies! My requests for information in the local papers and various parish magazines produced an amazing response. Everyone, it seemed, either had a privy or knew of one, or had a good story to tell.

On a warm summer's day the idea of trotting down the garden path, book in hand, to spend a pleasant half hour in the little stone building with the wooden seat seemed most appealing. On a freezing day in January, with the wind whistling around my ears, I was grateful for indoor sanitation!

My researches took me on a voyage of discovery to places I had never been to before and brought information about matters of which I previously had no knowledge. I discovered to my amazement that when I was a Beatle-mad teenager in the Swinging Sixties, there were people in rural Gloucestershire who were still using the old privy down the garden.

Some, indeed, have been in use far more recently than

that. Patrick Bird wrote to tell me of the family farm near Street in Somerset. 'There has never been a water closet at the farm. The family living there did not believe in change. Indeed the only concession to modern comforts has been a few electric light bulbs and a cold water tap in the kitchen. Consequently the privy survives, but maybe not for much longer.' A similarly unaltered farm at Downend, surrounded by modern houses next to a dual carriageway, is now being modernised, and its privy too may not last much longer.

Many have survived, however, and seem to be well loved and well looked after. I have recorded 85, and been told of about a dozen more which I hope to visit in the future. If yours does not appear in this book, I apologise; lack of space, not lack of interest, is responsible.

Linda Hall

[1]

A Short History of Loos

Privy comes originally from privy chamber, meaning a private room, and was a common term in medieval England. Others were necessarium, from the Latin for 'a necessary place'; or necessary house; jakes; gong; draught or withdraught; and garderobe. More recent terms include Houses of Parliament and penny house.

The earliest reference to a 'privy' of any sort comes in the Bible. The book of Samuel (Chapter 24) tells the story of King Saul hunting for David in the desert, intending to kill him. Saul 'came to a cave . . . and went in to relieve himself.' David and his men were hiding at the back of the cave, but instead of harming Saul, David crept over and cut off a piece of Saul's robe without him noticing. Saul must have been very engrossed in what he was doing not to notice all the whispering, let alone David's approach!

Civilisation is sometimes seen in terms of running water and inside loos, and on that reckoning the Romans are regarded as civilised in a way that did not happen again until the mid 19th century. Roman towns, villas and forts provide plentiful evidence of sophisticated water systems, and with that came latrines flushed by running water. The famous baths at Bath had a latrine which was flushed by the outlet from the circular bath, and many villas such as Chedworth and Wortley (near Wotton-under-Edge) had their own bathhouse complete with latrine. Piped rainwater flowed through an open gutter for rinsing out the sponges on sticks which they used instead of loo paper.

A Roman latrine – note the open-fronted seats for inserting the sponge sticks which were then washed in the small channels of running water in the floor.

At Olveston Court, the shaft from the garderobe discharged into the moat.

After the Romans left in the 5th century AD their civilised engineering works gradually fell out of use. Nothing is known of sanitary arrangements in the so-called Dark Ages, and the earliest evidence comes from the 12th century, after the Norman Conquest, when garderobes were built into the thickness of stone castle walls. Garderobe literally means wardrobe, and was the medieval equivalent of referring to the loo as the cloakroom. Excavated examples at Bristol Castle included fruit stones among their contents, suggesting that the garrison had a reasonably healthy diet. Berkeley Castle had similar garderobes in the curtain walls, while in the guardroom is what is believed to be a medieval urinal.

Thornbury Castle, left unfinished when the Duke of Buckingham was beheaded by Henry VIII in 1521, has garderobes spacious enough to be turned into modern

The prominent garderobe turret at Ostbridge Manor Farm, Pilning, a very fine 16th-century farmhouse.

bathrooms serving the bedrooms of what is now a luxury hotel. When Henry VIII and Anne Boleyn decided to visit Acton Court at Iron Acton in 1535, the owner Nicholas Poyntz must have felt rather apprehensive. Poyntz virtually rebuilt his old moated manor house in the most up-to-date style so that it would be fit to receive his majesty; he had no wish to follow the Duke of Buckingham to the block! The new east range, which still stands, included a series of grand state apartments on the first floor; the projecting chimney stacks also housed garderobes for the comfort of their occupants. Rumour had it that one was extra large to accommodate the king's great size, but in fact they are all the same size. Presumably Henry was satisfied with his accommodation, and Poyntz was knighted soon afterwards.

A few of the more substantial farmhouses also had garderobes, housed in projecting turrets, as the walls were not thick enough to accommodate them. They usually served the best bedroom, used by the owner and his wife. At Algar's Manor, Iron Acton, the 16th-century garderobe tower was enlarged, probably in the 17th century, and now contains a WC! Various medieval garderobes have been excavated in Bristol, including the unusual semi-circular garderobe turret at Westbury College, rebuilt between 1455 and 1475 by Bishop Carpenter of Worcester. The evidence of blocked doorways shows that the 17th-century house in Lower Park Row, recently restored, had a three-storey privy block, which may have been timber-framed. Other houses in the city have 'multi-storey blocks . . . of very limited floor area' which were probably privy blocks.

Medieval monasteries were always at the forefront of water supply and sanitation, and Bristol was no exception. A substantial stone culvert south of the cathedral has evidence for a privy built over it, and there is another on the site of the

11

Franciscan Friary in Lewins Mead. Archaeologists in the city have also found medieval and later cesspools built of Pennant sandstone, with vaulted roofs and flagstone floors, but we do not know what sort of structure covered them. One at Greyfriars contained leather shoes with fashionable pointed toes, inscribed slates used by students in the friary school, and wooden bowls and platters, all from around 1500; they survived due to the waterlogged conditions.

Later cesspits contain items such as glass wine bottles, stoneware tankards from the Rhineland, delft-ware chamber pots and unbroken clay pipes. The last item is surprising, as the fragility of the long thin stem of a clay pipe makes it unlikely to survive the fall down the shaft and remain intact. Was someone perhaps enjoying a quiet smoke in the privacy of the garderobe, only to drop the pipe down the hole? A later cesspit on St Michael's Hill contained the broken remains of 18th and 19th-century chamber pots, including one of tin-glazed earthenware from Bristol itself and another made in Staffordshire. If they were broken around the house, the privy would be the natural place to dispose of the pieces, or was the family plagued by careless servants who kept dropping chamber pots down the shaft when emptying them?

The cesspit was designed to be emptied by the 'night soil men', known as 'gong fermers' in medieval times. They were, quite rightly, highly paid for doing this most unpleasant task, but sometimes their employer also paid someone to keep an eye on them to make sure they did their job properly! Other pits were built as dead wells, to be filled and then covered, with a new pit built nearby. These could cause trouble long after their existence had been forgotten. In his book *Clean and Decent* Lawrence Wright tells of a late 19th-century plumber, working by the light of a candle; as he lifted one of the flagstones in the floor he was blown up by the gases escaping from a forgotten cesspit. Medieval dyers' houses in Redcliff Street had pits for large vats to hold both stale urine and water – the urine was used instead of Fuller's Earth for cleaning the cloth, and the water for rinsing afterwards. Quite how the urine was collected is not known!

Bristol seems to have been far more pleasant and less unsavoury than many Elizabethan towns. As early as 1480, William of Worcester mentioned 'a privey both for women and men' in Bristol, and other public conveniences were known in London, Exeter, Winchester, Southampton and Hull. The late 16th-century writer William Camden commented on the cleanliness of Bristol, while in 1634 some soldiers remarked that 'The City is very sweet and cleane in respect of the quotidian [daily] tydes that wash and cleanse her lower part, and the vaults and sewers that are under all'. The unusually large rise and fall of the tide at Bristol was clearly of great benefit.

Across the Severn at Tintern Abbey the monks' reredorter, or privy block, was also flushed by the action of the tide, which flowed up the River Wye from the Severn. Before it was demolished in 1761, Bristol Bridge was lined with five-storey timber houses, and old drawings show some with small timber projections, presumably privies emptying directly into the river.

Unfortunately the construction of the floating harbour in 1809 meant that the tides no longer cleaned the rivers Avon and Frome, and the centre of the city became exceedingly smelly and unpleasant. Combined with the huge increase in population this led to a very high death rate in the mid 19th century. In 1845 a *Report on the Sanatory Condition of Bristol* painted an extremely unpleasant picture of life in the city. and 34 sewers discharged directly into the floating harbour.

When the waters were low in summer and autumn the poor people who lived along the river said that it made them 'turn sick'. Even in Clifton 'the want of proper sewerage is deplorable. Ranges of handsome houses . . . have nothing but a system of cesspools . . . There is indeed a sewer down two-thirds of the Royal Crescent . . .' as well as in many of the other streets.

Some of the wealthier houses had water closets by this time, but in the poorer areas the privies were rarely cleaned, and by 1889 the houses were so densely packed that 'privies actually exist in living rooms'. Many of the wells in the city were contaminated with sewage, in contrast to the 16th century when Bristol was noted for its good supply of clean water. Things began to improve when the Bristol Water Works Company was set up in 1846 to provide clean water, while the Sanitary Committee started to improve the drains.

Matters were not quite so bad in Bath, where substantial drains were provided during the Georgian rebuilding of the town. Despite the new drains, however, nasty accidents sometimes happened. In 1763 the *Bath Chronicle* reported an accident in Westgate Street. 'Three men, having dug a hole adjoining to a necessary house, in order to empty it, the contents rushed in so suddenly upon two of them that they were immediately suffocated. The third man went to their assistance and shared the same fate.' Some houses in Bath had privies in their basements, probably used by the servants rather than the family.

The flush toilet has a remarkably long history, and is not the modern invention which people often believe. The first flushing water closet in England was invented by Sir John Harington in 1596; he installed one for his godmother,

Queen Elizabeth I, at Richmond Palace in Surrey, and built another at his own home, Kelston Manor near Bath. The manor house was in the field next to the churchyard, and on the wall is a memorial tablet to Sir John and other members of his family. While I was looking at this, an elderly local resident came over and asked if I would like to see something of interest. He showed me an iron door in the wall on the west side of the raised churchyard, which led to an underground water channel. Presumably this was part of Sir John's water system, which fed ornamental fountains and fish ponds as well as the water closet.

Sir John Harington was ahead of his time, however; in most places the water supply was not sophisticated enough to cope with water closets and the idea was not developed. Letters between the architect John Wood and the Duke of Chandos in 1727 talk of providing ten water closets in St John's hospital in Bath, and when Wood designed Prior Park Mansion in 1735 he included a basement room under the portico for water closets if they were required. No one knows if any were actually installed, however. Plans for the Bristol Corn Exchange, built in the 1740s, show 21 separate 'bog houses' inside the building, as well as water pipes, implying that these were water flushed. Even more remarkable is the diagram in the *Kings Weston Book of Drawings* (architects' drawings from the 1720s and 1730s) which shows a ballcock in what looks very like a modern cistern.

The first patent for a water closet was taken out in 1775 by Alexander Cummings, a London watchmaker. Three years later Joseph Bramah patented an improved model with an efficient valve, which was better at eliminating foul smells, and he claimed to have made 6,000 by 1797. An original Bramah is still in use in the House of Lords in London. By the 1780s it was quite common for townhouses to have

Privies built out over the River Frome in the centre of Bristol; these contributed to the appalling conditions prevalent in the 19th century.

The basement privy in an early 19th-century house in Woodland Place, Bath. The walls of the cubicle are built of large blocks of Bath stone, and a slate tank is perched above to give some sort of flushing system.

indoor WCs, and improved water supplies enabled them to be sited upstairs as well as down. The water suppliers were not always happy about the situation, however, as the water closets of the time used far more water than modern examples. Piped water was regarded as being for drinking, and it was far too wasteful to use it for flushing WCs. In 1770 the suppliers threatened to cut off the water supply of a Mr Melmouth of Bladud Buildings in Bath unless he stopped using it for his WC. In some houses rainwater was used instead.

These new designs of water closet, supposedly free from unpleasant smells, were advertised in the *Bath Chronicle and Weekly Gazette* in 1789 as being suitable for installation 'in any parlour, bedroom or dressing room'. The adverts were aimed at 'the Nobility, Gentry and Builders', but whether the

Joseph Bramah's valve closet was the accepted WC pattern for almost 100 years after it was first introduced in 1778. The mechanism was housed in wooden casing.

Catherine Place in Bath, where two houses have a cantilevered loo block added on the back of the building. (Photo by Tony Crouch)

products lived up to the claims is another matter. By the 1860s all new houses were expected to have water closets, and they were added to many existing buildings. Sometimes people were not able to have water closets, not because they were too expensive, but because their water supply was not good enough. This was the case out in the country at Badminton House, where commodes for the women and earth closets for the men were in use until 1917.

The true earth closet was the invention of the Rev. Henry Moule as an alternative to the flushing toilet or the cesspit, although people commonly use the term when referring to a privy with a vault. A hopper was fixed above the pan, containing fine earth or ash, and when a handle was pulled up it released the earth to cover the contents of the pan. Mrs.

19

MOULE'S EARTH CLOSETS

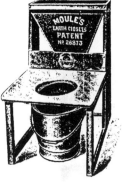

Apparatus on Bearers ready to Fix.
Deal Seat 3' 0" Long.

No. A1724. " Pull Out," as drawn.
No. A1725. " Pull Up " Pattern.
No. A1726. " Self-acting " Pattern.

Strong, Portable, Self-Contained Set. Plain Deal. Galvanized Fittings. Pail complete. 21" Wide. 27" Back to Front.

No. A1727. " Pull Out."
(as drawn)
No. A1728. " Pull Up "

Strong, Portable, Self-contained.
Best Plain Deal.
Fittings of Galvanized Iron.
With Pail complete.

No. A1729. Self-Acting. 21" Wide.
27" Back to Front. 36" High.

No.		
A1724	..	.. 57/6
A1725	..	.. 70/-
A1726	..	.. 100/-
*A1727	..	.. 72/6
*A1728	..	.. 86/6
*A1729	..	.. 102/6

* Pails included.
Other Pails **3/7** Each Extra.

First patented in 1860, the Rev Henry Moule's earth closets were still popular at the outbreak of World War II. This ironmonger's catalogue of 1936 includes the automatic or 'self-acting' model (bottom).

Mrs Minchin has an impressive collection of chamber pots, shown here on the well outside her home in North Road, Yate.

Beard of Woodford remembers one in use at Green Farm, Falfield, where she lived about fifty years ago. I have not found any in the area, nor been told of any others, so it may be that they were never very common in this part of the world.

Chamber pots and close stools were used at night to save people from making the long cold trek down the garden path. Close stools were pewter chamber pots enclosed in a wooden box seat, an early version of the commode. These were nearly always in bedrooms, and in the late 18th century a house in the Royal Crescent in Bath had a mahogany 'night stool' in the front garret. Sometimes separate closets were provided; a sales prospectus for a merchant's house in Bristol in 1724 includes 'Two large dark closets, which may have light over their doors from the staircase window and will be of great convenience for the holding of close stools and many other family necessarys'.

Chamber pots remained popular for night-time use well into the 20th century, and the late Frank Gastrell, who wrote his *Almondsbury Memories* in 1980, has some amusing stories to tell. Young couples setting up home would buy a set of bedroom ware, consisting of two chamber pots, wash basin and jug, and soap dish, all available in various colours and decoration. 'The chamber pots would be kept under the bed. The contents of such pots have been known to have been thrown out of the window to cool the ardour of courting couples below who were taking a long time to say goodnight!'

Michael Clinch writes that 'the visit to the top of the garden was of course a ritual in the morning to empty the chamber pot, discreetly covered by its small towel'. Gwynne Stock of Tormarton recalls that 'the outside facilities were augmented (and fed) by chamber pots, via a 'slop bucket' – a white enamel bucket with a lid like a very shallow fluted funnel, with a small enamel dome over a central hole. The steam from a pot under the bed could cause bed-springs and frames to rust, and the contents were a good indicator of temperature, when a shim of ice was present in the morning.' Brrrr!

[2]

Up the Garden Path

Out in the countryside large gardens and spacious farmyards gave ample room for the detached privy. The earliest surviving privy buildings date from the 17th century, when it appears that people grew tired of living with a smelly garderobe inside the house, preferring instead to put the loo down the garden. Certainly the garderobe at The Manor House, Gaunts Earthcott was superseded by an outside privy, as a small stone building close to the house almost certainly started life as such. This in turn was replaced by a brick-built privy further away in a corner of the garden. It was still in existence when Julian and Diana St John Brooks moved in in the 1950s, but they dismantled it and used the bricks as edging for the flower beds and garden paths. The site is now a very fertile compost heap!

One of the earliest privies, at Moorend Farm, Hambrook, is known to the locals as 'Cromwell's Bog' in the belief that Oliver Cromwell once used it. As it dates from the 17th century, Cromwell could, in theory at least, have used it; he was certainly in the area during the Civil War in the mid 17th century. It is a substantial building, divided into two rooms, with seats for three adults and two lower seats for children. One set of seats could be original; its construction uses larger and older-looking planks than the other. Below the seats is a deep pit, with a wide arch in the rear wall for emptying it, and a recess in each end wall could have held a candle.

All of the earliest privies are built of local stone, with roofs of either the S-shaped pantiles or double Roman tiles, both

Melton Farm, Lower Stone. A typical free-standing privy with a pitched roof and a double seat.

made in the Bridgwater area. Occasionally slate is used instead. Many are free-standing with pitched roofs, so that they do indeed look like a 'Small House', one of the euphemisms for the privy. Equally common is the single pitched roof , on both lean-to and on free-standing privies. There is a huge variety of building stone available in the Bristol region; red or grey Pennant sandstone in Bristol itself and in the Winterbourne-Iron Acton area; thin slabs of golden lias limestone in Pucklechurch and Stoke Gifford; chunky blocks of pink and grey carboniferous limestone in Almondsbury, Tockington and Olveston; and of course the well-known oolitic limestone towards the Cotswold scarp, including the famous Bath stone. Houses, farm buildings and privies are all built of the nearest available stone, as to transport it any distance increased the costs enormously. The walls can be anything up to eighteen inches thick and often contain a recess for the candle. The earliest windows were simple unglazed slits; later ones were larger and had glazing. Where the better quality oolitic limestone was available, large squared blocks were used for corner stones and doorways, as in the late 18th-century privy at Castle Farm, Marshfield. It is a pit type, with a two-holed seat with hinged lids, a plaster ceiling and a window with leaded lights. I have also been told of a magnificent privy at Corston built entirely of Bath stone.

I have noted about 20 brick privies, all built between the late 18th and the early 20th century; many are in the area around Hill, Rockhampton and Slimbridge, where brick houses of this period are common. Many are quite small, often only about four feet wide, but the one at Furzedown Farm, Tockington is over six feet square. Stone privies can be equally large, but the smallest is the little lean-to at Pauline Preddy's home in Wellow. This measures only two feet by about three feet inside, giving just enough room for the WC,

'Cromwell's Bog' – the amazing 17th-century two-roomed privy at Moorend Farm, Hambrook *(Top)* The possibly original seat surviving in one of the cubicles. *(Bottom)* The three seats in the second cubicle, with an assortment of lids.

26

A substantial and well-built privy at Castle Farm, Marshfield. Large blocks of Bath stone frame the door and the window, and the roof is slate. This is where the postman got the fright of his life (see Chapter 8)!

and is rather like the extremely cramped cubicles provided at some motorway service stations! Its walls have been raised so that the height is now more comfortable than the original 4' 5" at the back and 5' 7" at the door. Many privy doors are in fact quite low, well under six feet and sometimes as low as five feet. Were people shorter, or did they just get used to ducking?

Ken and Eileen Prout have lived in Chipping Sodbury for about 40 years, in a house believed to date back to 1690. The tiny stone privy at the side of the garden may be the same age; it has a pantile roof, a five-foot doorway and no window. It had a cesspit at the side and, according to the neighbours, the previous owners used the contents to feed a vine in the greenhouse. The WC which replaced it is in a small brick building just outside the back door and reached by a covered porch. It is much the same size as the original privy. Indoors they have a camping toilet for night-time use, and, being a keen gardener, Ken uses the contents to activate his compost heap!

Eileen was born at Engine Common, where they had a bucket privy, and later lived in North Road in Yate, where they had a two-seater (same level) privy. The buckets were emptied into a cesspit which also took the water from all the sinks. Ken was born in nearby Chaingate Lane where they had a galvanised privy, also the bucket type, down the garden. Nearer the house was an older stone-built privy; when he and Eileen married in 1940 the house was divided in two and his father did up the old stone privy for his own use. Presumably this entailed the purchase of a new bucket. I don't know if any of these privies have survived, but the area has proved a fruitful one – I have been to three privies in Chaingate Lane and two in North Road, and there may well be more waiting to be discovered.

Many privies were sited a long way 'down the garden' or 'up the garden', being built against the boundary wall or hedge at the end. This could be a long trek, especially in the sort of unpleasant weather that I encountered when recording the privy at Ivory Hill Farm. The late Mrs Watts referred to this old privy as the 'Penny House' and said it was 'a blinking nuisance' having to go all the way down the garden! In Acton Turville Freda Brown lived at Rose Cottage until about ten years ago, where as a child she sometimes used to ride her bike down the long garden to save walking. Janet Drew's mother also used to ride to the privy, but this was due to necessity – she suffered badly from rheumatoid arthritis and was confined to a wheelchair. When they moved to North Road, Yate in 1957 her husband relaid the old ash path with concrete to make it easier for her, but it is still amazing to think that she managed to propel herself down

The privy in the garden of Ken and Eileen Prout's house in Chipping Sodbury.
To the right was the cesspit where their nephew fell in (see Chapter 8).

The 'Penny House' at Ivory Hill Farm, Kendleshire.

the garden several times a day. He also widened the privy doorway, converted it from a pit to a bucket and had a new lift-up seat made; it was a single-holer, with a separate lid with a knob handle. The walls were painted with yellow distemper and the privy remained in use until the mains sewers came at the end of the 1960s.

Privies may be attached to other buildings; the ruined privy at Rock House, Elberton is on the back of the detached bakehouse, while a cottage in Olveston has a lean-to privy on the end of the Methodist chapel. At a farm near Bitton, the privy is on the back of the cowshed opposite the back door of the house, and there is a back-to-back privy in a similar position at Home Farm in Hawkesbury Upton. By far the most common site is next to the pigsty – I can only assume that the smell from one masked the smell from the other!

30

[3]

RATS AND CREEPY CRAWLIES

Animals of one sort or another featured in many people's memories of 'going up the garden', and could cause a lot of alarm to, dare I say it, the women and children! Walter Ford of Elberton told me that they all used to kick the door of the 'Small House' before going in, to make sure that any rats who may have been inside did not remain so. Otherwise, the men have maintained a stoical silence on the subject of wildlife! Children in particular tended to dislike the various creepy crawlies which lived in the average privy. Vera White's comments were typical: 'As children we weren't too keen on seeing the garden spiders that had a habit of going in the 'loo'. We were always told they were quite friendly!'

North Road, Yate was full of wildlife, as June Broom recalls. 'I can remember going up the garden path with a torch late at night, with all the spiders and woodlice running around the floor because they came out at night.' Mrs. Hale also used to find the privy seat covered in woodlice, but 'they seemed to disappear pretty quickly with the light'. She also remembers being scared of the noises the cows made when they were close to the privy, and Maureen Moras remembers the cows in the field behind the privy making her jump when they coughed.

For another of my correspondents, Carole, the experience was rather more dramatic and deserves to be told in full! 'It seems so funny to me now but at the time it was horrendously frightening. It was the middle of winter during the late 1960s. I was visiting my boyfriend's delightful cottage in the country. Because of its remoteness there were no drainage facilities – just the old 'bucket and chuckit' as the old privy was fondly known! In the winter or when raining, one tended to 'hang on' and put off the necessary journey outside for as long as possible! On one such evening, more than ready to 'excuse' myself, I lifted the latch on the back door and thrust myself out into the blustery air. As the privy was all but a few yards away I didn't bother to take a torch. As soon as I entered and took my seat, I was frightened to death by a sudden huge husky cough sound. Thinking my doom was nigh, I hurried my task, felt for the privy door latch, when spontaneously something that felt very coarse and resistant literally brushed my forehead and over my hair. I was absolutely petrified. I can't remember my hasty retreat back to the safety of the cottage! As I reached the door, the dreadful sound abruptly filled the air once more. It was at this point that I realised it was a cow coughing in the field over the hedge that was just feet away from the privy. Out of breath and completely stunned I panted out my ordeal. My boyfriend explained that the scary head-brushing experience was caused only by a hessian sack that was pinned up above the large gap over the privy door. 'We always have that there during the winter to keep out the north wind.' . . . wish he'd told me before . . . Yes, I did marry him!'

Mrs Pope at Cripps Farm, St Catherine also had a bovine encounter in the dark. The house has a rear wing containing the dairy, and the little lean-to privy is built onto the end wall. Late one night Mrs Pope found a large black cow lying with its backside firmly up against the back door. She kicked and prodded it but it refused to move, so in desperation she clambered over the sleeping beast with only the light of a small torch to see by. She achieved her mission, then climbed back over the animal which still had not moved. The next

Mrs Pope on the site of her encounter with a large black bull on a late-night trip to the privy at her home at Cripps Farm, St Catherine.

morning she looked out of the window to see that the cow was still lying in its sheltered spot by the back door – only by the light of day she could see that it was in fact a large bull! 'I was scared stiff when I saw it,' she told me. She also remembered The Sandybanks pub at St Catherine, which before it closed in 1966 still had Ladies' and Gents' privies. On one occasion there was a sign saying that the Ladies' was out of action as a fox had a litter of cubs in there and could not be disturbed. A friend recalled that the Gents' had no seat, only a wooden trough. 'Usually we didn't bother,' he said, 'we just used to pee over the wall!'

Other animals occasionally featured in people's stories. Sandra Broomsgrove told me of a lady at Little Badminton who, when a child, went out to the privy and was terrified by a snake which slithered in under the door. She jumped up onto the seat, screaming, and then dashed indoors where her father asked her what on earth was the matter. When she told her parents, her mother answered that it could have been worse: 'You could have gone down into the hole, what with the woodworm in the seat!' Local historian David Tandy was told another snake story by a lady from Newport, whose father one day brought home a dead snake to show her mother. He then disposed of the body down the privy. His daughter must have thought that it was not really dead, as she refused to use the privy for three days! She did not say what she used instead; perhaps the privy next door. Some children were more resilient, however, and Mavis Gill of Alveston 'got a concertina and played it to keep the rat at bay' when the animal frightened her mother near the privy.

[4]

ONE, TWO AND THREE HOLERS

About a quarter of the 85 privies I have visited still have their wooden seats intact. A few have a single hole, but most common are the two-holers, usually with one large and one slightly smaller hole at the same level. As Patrick Bird comments, 'it has never been clear whether this is a male/female or adult/child arrangement.' (And if it was male/female, who had the larger bottom?) More obvious are those few privies where the child's seat is at a lower level, but this seems to have been less common than one might expect. Mary Hardwick remembers that this was the arrangement at Hall End Farm near Wickwar before the seats were removed and the building turned into a coalshed. Gwynne Stock remembers another such privy, now gone, at the former Post Office Stores in Tormarton. 'The seating was of scrubbed wood, and was a "two holer/two size/two level", and graduation from the junior to the senior level was a proud moment,' he recalls.

An unusual arrangement survives in the 18th-century privy at St Arild's Farm at Kington, near Thornbury. Here the adult two-holer has a tiny child's seat set at right angles to it, with a carved armrest to stop the child falling off sideways. The builders of this privy went to a lot of trouble, as the candle recess below the window has a wooden frame with a tiny moulding around the edge; usually these recesses are a plain hole in the wall with a simple wooden lintel. Three-holers are rare, although several people remember them, as well as a couple of four-holers. Charles Eardley-Wilmott of

The author's daughter Catherine inspects the child's seat at Moorend Farm, Hambrook.

At Bromley Heath Farm, Downend, the candle recess in the privy is still very much in use, with drips of wax down the wall and sooty marks above the charred lintel.

37

The child's seat, complete with armrest, in the 18th-century three-seater at St Arild's Farm, Kington.

Lower Morton told me of a pub at Bevington, 'The Rampant Cat' (in reality sometimes like 'The Red Lion' I imagine!), which had either a three or a five-holer in use in recent years, but I have been unable to locate it. Nellie Garland remembered a three-seater on three different levels at West Horrington near Wells, while the late Mrs Watts of Ivory Hill Farm, Kendleshire, remembered a three-seater where they used to live in Somerset; she said it reminded her of Mummy Bear, Daddy Bear and Baby Bear!

Many seats are extremely spacious, perhaps because they were indeed intended for two or even three people to sit there companionably side by side. The front of the seat is usually constructed of wooden planks, but sometimes brick is used instead. At Mrs Climmer's privy in Winterbourne Down the seat was made of stone. The slab of Pennant has a rather irregular hole cut into it, and it was supported on a wooden framework; this was open at the front for removal of the white enamel bucket, but perhaps once had a door. The elderly gentleman and his sister who lived there were still using the privy in 1983. To alleviate the cold, they had covered the seat with a blanket, the strategically placed hole stitched neatly around the edge.

The hole in this stone seat is surrounded by a slightly recessed area, presumably to take a square wooden lid. Quite a number of circular wooden lids survive, and most have two neat finger holes cut in the centre. Sometimes wooden battens are fixed to the top to make a handle, and in Littleton Maureen Moras's mother remembers asking for a lid with a brass knob when hers had to be replaced. A few privies have hinged lids, and this may be a later feature, perhaps dating from the 19th century. Many seats have of course been replaced over the years, and it is doubtful whether any 17th-century examples survive except for the

The front of the double seat at Ivory Hill Farm, Kendleshire is a single slab of Pennant sandstone.

You had to be extra hardy to use this privy at Winterbourne Down, as the actual seat was made of stone! It now leans against the wall at the bottom of the garden.

one at Moorend Farm (Chapter 2). Peggy James in Olveston needed a new seat sometime in the late 1950s, and recalls drawing a template on a large sheet of paper, which she then took to the carpenter. Although most seats consist simply of a plank of wood with one or more round or oval holes in it, a few have been fitted with some sort of pan beneath the hole, as at Hill House in Olveston and Kingswood in Bristol. Cotham House in Olveston has an unusual seat, probably replacing an earlier wooden one. Here the almost square seat base has a concrete top containing a central depression. At the bottom of this are the broken remains of a china pan, which flushed away (with a bucket of water?) to a cesspit at the side of the privy.

Arrangements below the seat varied. The oldest seems to be the deep pit or vault with a hole for emptying it either in the side or the back. These holes are often square or rectangular with either a stone or a wooden lintel, but some were larger with a stone or brick arch. They would have been filled in loosely with stone or brick until the time came for emptying; alternatively earth would have been piled against the opening to absorb the moisture and leave a relatively savoury dry deposit to be dug out. Some pits were designed to channel the material into a cesspit behind the privy, where the liquid could soak away. In these cases the sides of the pit may slope down from floor level, as at Melton Farm at Lower Stone and Jacob's Well at Oldbury. The cesspit was a potential hazard; June Broom recalled that theirs had a wooden lid, while at Hall End Farm the pit was covered with thick branches to keep the cattle out, as the privy backs onto a field.

The third type of privy had a bucket or buckets, removed either through a trapdoor or via a lift-up seat (see Chapter 7). It is not always clear whether a privy began life with a vault

This privy at Dapps Hill, Keynsham is built beside rather than over the stream. There are steps down to the stream so that whoever used the privy could fill a bucket with water to flush it.

or a bucket, but if a privy is built across a slope, so that the side or the back wall descends well below floor level, then it almost certainly started off as a vault privy, even if the arch or emptying hole has been so well filled in that nothing is visible. I found examples at The Elms at Rockhampton and in Station Road in Charfield, both brick privies built across a slope even though there was some perfectly level ground available. The fourth type was perhaps the most efficient, the privy built over running water. At Goosegreen Farm, Yate the large privy, possibly dating from the late 17th century, was built over a stream and was still in use in 1963. Since then the stream has dried up. So has the ditch at Champery in Mill Lane, Falfield. In 1978 when Mr and Mrs Pike moved in, the privy was just a shell covered in ivy, and the roof had fallen in.

The most unusual and probably the most efficient is at Cripps Farm, St Catherine's. Probably built around 1800, the house has a rear dairy wing with the lean-to privy on the end of it. When the Popes arrived in 1963 the house had only just had electricity installed and the privy was still in use. Indeed, as long as the seat could take the strain, it is still perfectly usable. It is flushed by water from two springs across the road, which is piped under the house into a tank in the old dairy. From here the overflow is piped through the wall to flush the privy. The water then flows to some sort of catch pit, from where the water emerges apparently pure. Judy Grant's house in Keynsham has its privy built next to a stream which tumbles down the hill into the river Chew. When they moved in a luridly coloured WC had been installed, but the Keynsham and Saltford Local History Society have a 1973 photo showing a square stone construction topped by a wooden seat. Next to it a galvanised bucket stands ready to flush it; it was filled from the stream, where several steps have been built down to the water for this purpose.

[5]

'BUCKET AND CHUCKIT'

Disposal of the contents was of course a major task for privy owners. Most properties in those days had gardens large enough to accommodate the trenches necessary for burying the ordure, while on farms it would be used to augment the muck heap. Not surprisingly, many of the people I met had vivid memories of this rather unpleasant job and of the superb vegetables which everyone grew as a result! Several mentioned tomatoes which grew where none had been planted, clear evidence that tomato pips pass unchanged through the human digestive system!

The method of disposal depended on the type of privy. If it was built over a stream or ditch, the water would carry the effluent away for you, although it must have been very unpleasant for anyone living downstream! The only maintenance required would be to ensure that nothing blocked the water supply. Bucket privies had a trapdoor in the wall either behind or beside the seat, or in the seat front; this was safer if there were mischievous people around who might use an outside door for unpleasant purposes (see Chapter 12)! The wooden doors were either hinged or could be lifted out and were held in place by a wooden turnbuckle on either side. It could be quite tricky to remove a full bucket through a trapdoor without spilling it, so sometimes the whole seat hinged up.

Mr Browning of Morton Mill recalls buying a 'steel' (galvanised?) privy bucket from the ironmonger back in the 1950s, while Michael Clinch remembers his parents' privy

The author with the privy bucket which she discovered in an old tin bath at Holm Farm, Pilning.

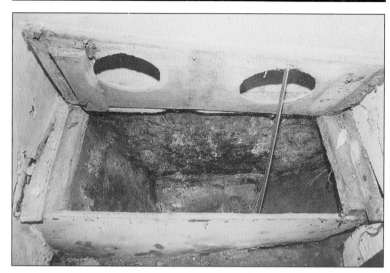

The vault below the seat and the remains of the phase one arch in the rear wall. It must have been very difficult to position a bucket correctly beneath either of the holes on account of the sloping sides of the pit at Melton Farm.

'with its accompanying vitreous enamel bucket with ventilated lid, which naughty boys might use as entry if they couldn't be bothered to take the lid off'. The buckets are a very distinctive shape, taller than a normal bucket and more sturdily built. They are oval, splayed out at the base for stability, and have a handle low down on the side to make the task of emptying easier and more accurate! A few have survived in odd corners of farmyards or doing duty as flower containers.

In larger villages and towns the buckets would have been emptied by men employed by the local council, who came round with what was popularly referred to as the lavender cart. In the cities, back alleys were provided to streets of terraced houses so that these brave souls could go about their task with the minimum of disturbance to the inhabitants. One such survives in Kingswood, where a pair of back-to-back privies survives behind a late Victorian terrace of three houses. Both privies retain their single-holed seats, one of them complete with a fitted pan below the wooden hole. To find a pair of privies still standing within a large city in the year 2000 must be rare indeed.

So far I have found few recollections of the bucket men, but Mavis Gill of Alveston recalls the strong smell when they came to her childhood home in Dorset. John Forster's grandparents lived in one of a terrace of four Georgian houses in Stock Lane in Berkeley, demolished in the 1960s; the brick single-holer privy had a pantiled roof and a sagging hessian ceiling. Here there was no back entrance to the garden, so when the man came round with his horse and cart to empty the privies, the contents had to be carried out through the house! It must have been most unpleasant for all concerned.

For most people, bucket emptying was very much a matter of do-it-yourself, and was usually a job done by the men, as Vera White recalls. In the late 1930s her grandparents lived at Tierley, near Bath. 'Granfer was in charge of bucket clearing; there was a wooden door on the back wall and we children were frequently warned about the two holes in the garden, one for lavatory and the other for household waste water. I must say the vegetables always looked healthy and strong; Granfer was always proud of them!' Michael Clinch has vivid memories of his father and his grandfather digging trenches on a Saturday morning in their Olveston gardens. 'The bucket's contents would be lovingly placed in the trench and the next few spade spits would be dug to cover up the precious contents which brought plentiful harvests all through the seasons.' In the same village, Mr. Hicks was grateful not to have been older and stronger. 'The job of emptying it fell to my late father, as my late brother and I were not deemed to be big enough to carry out this job and we did not argue this point.'

The belief that a bucket privy was superior to the pit type was also voiced by Jack Walters of Marshfield. He remembers the old school privies as 'de luxe models with buckets!' Nellie Garland expressed the opposite point of view. Her grandparents' house was at West Horrington near Wells. 'The wood privy was on three levels, with three holes, with wooden lids on them, and in the corner was an old churn filled with lime, and after performing you put some lime down the hole and put the lid on again. This was considered quite posh in those days; most houses had a bucket privy which had to be emptied each week in a hole dug in the garden. My Dad used to put the chicken manure in as well and when dug in the garden, made everything grow like mad.'

Emptying the privy could prove unpleasant for both the family and the neighbours. Buckets had to be emptied every week, or possibly more often in the case of large families. People developed their own routines, which did not necessarily meet with approval next door. In Littleton-on-Severn Maureen Moras's dad used to come back home for his breakfast after working on the farm early on a Sunday morning. Unfortunately their neighbour chose exactly this time to empty his bucket; the smells wafting across the garden must have taken the edge off his appetite! He preferred to empty their bucket on a Sunday evening. Someone else remembered a vault privy in Britannia Road, Kingswood; when her grandfather cleared it out twice a year, the smell was so overpowering that everybody moved out for the day.

To empty a vault some sort of long-handled tool was

This pair of late 19th-century back-to-back privies in Kingswood, Bristol would have been emptied by the bucket men coming along the back alley.

49

needed to reach into the depths of the pit and to keep the smelly contents as far away from the person doing the job as possible. Some people improvised a tool for the job. In Yate Mrs Hale's father used a long stick with an old saucepan on the end, and he used to burn some old rags to try and mask the smell. Being 'a very fastidious man' he used to dig an extremely deep pit, and he strongly disapproved of his sister and brother-in-law next door, who were far less particular and only dug a relatively shallow trench. Other people borrowed a scoop when the time came to clean out their privy. Mary Knight remembers with amusement that their grandparents at Mill Farm, Siston Common used to borrow a long-handled dip from other members of the family at Wick. She remembers them driving back to Mill Farm with it sticking out of the sunshine roof of the car!

Gwynne Stock described a privy in Tormarton. 'This privy, of the earth closet variety, was up the garden, a distance of some twelve yards. The pit access was just outside the building, covered with stout planks, and lay within a quarter circle of a high dry stone boundary wall. It was emptied from time to time, after dark, in lantern light, by two chain-smoking men. The contents were transferred by scoop and bucket to a trench in the garden – the process no doubt accounted for the excellent crops of runner beans. The progress of the shadowy figures could additionally be followed by the bobbing glow of the cigarettes. The time for emptying was signalled by a pyramid of the contents approaching the top (and the bottom!).' The chain smoking presumably helped to mask the awful smell. As Reg Howlett recorded in *Staple Hill; A History*, 'You needed a poor sense of smell and a strong sense of humour.'

Often the privy contents were added to the muck from the stables, pigsties and cowsheds before being used as fertiliser.

A special long-handled scoop was used to empty the privy.

As Sarah Spratt of Alveston recalls, 'Being very young at that time I am not very knowledgeable about how it was emptied but I presume it was treated the same way as the cowshed, calfpen and piggeries and spread on the arable fields! I do remember one year seeing very small tomatoes ripening after the corn had been harvested!' Bottoms Farm (a rather appropriate name!) has the remains of a lean-to privy set into the garden wall at the end of a row of pigsties. The farmer, Richard Hudson, told me that in the late 19th century, drainage was put in for the whole farmyard. This ran into a septic tank, and the privy was linked up to this system so that it no longer had to be laboriously emptied. June Broom recalled that the lime and ash added by each user meant that it was not actually unpleasant to clean out the privy as the contents resembled compost from a compost heap. Her dad took it in his wheelbarrow to add to the muck heap along with the manure from the pigs and the horses.

The privy at Melton Farm, Lower Stone was still used daily by the elderly gentleman who lived there until about 1994. He used to empty the bucket into the ditch which ran along the back of the privy into the slurry pit, which also took all the run-off from the cowsheds and the pigsties. Despite the fact that he had no indoor toilet, he had a bath installed in the house, but although the water inlets were properly plumbed in, the outlets were not! When he had finished his bath, the water went out through a pipe straight through the wall of the house and emptied over the garden.

[6]

WHATEVER THE WEATHER

Many people have memories connected with the weather which make the medieval name of 'the draught' or 'the withdraught' seem particularly appropriate. Michael Clinch recalls, 'The violent accompanying freezing up-draughts of cold air in the winter would chill to the marrow, and visits were always brief and only accomplished when entirely necessary.' Mrs Vera White of Freshford also used to make her trips up the garden as short as possible. 'Another reason why my visits were in haste was the fact it could be draughty at

June Broom was amazed when reunited with her childhood privy in Yate: 'No one's been in here for forty years! It's hard to believe I was once small enough to sit on that seat!'

times sitting upon the 'throne' where the winds came through the door whereby Granfer removed the bucket.' Mary Knight remembers the 'good cross current of draughts', while another of my correspondents described a privy built over a stream at Kilcott as 'VERY draughty but very efficient!' June Broom has similar memories of the old privy which still stands, now completely overgrown, at the end of her mother's garden in North Road, Yate. 'You didn't stay long because it was so draughty.'

Maureen Moras also lives next door to her childhood home, Lynch House in Littleton, and has vivid memories of the privy which has no window and no ventilation hole in the door. It should have been snug, but Maureen remembers it as 'very airy'. This was because the roof had no insulation

The pigsty with the privy behind it at Mr Amos's cottage in Doynton. This was where he remembers shovelling snow off the seat before using it. The enormously long garden still seems very productive after years of burying bucketfuls of you-know-what!

beneath the pantiles, and their S-shaped profile allows plenty of draughts in underneath. And not only air. Mr Amos, a sprightly 88-year-old, has memories to make us grateful for indoor facilities and central heating! Winters seemed to be harder when he moved to Doynton some fifty years ago, and they often had two or three feet of snow covering the back garden. Consequently they always kept a shovel, a brush and a pair of wellies in the back porch ready for the trip to the privy. Luckily it was only a few yards from the back door, next to the pigsty, but they often had to shovel the snow off the seat before they could use it, as it had blown in under the pantiles! 'It could be very eerie in winter with the wind howling around,' he said.

Mary Hulbert used to live in Tockington, where 'the privy was still in use when my father moved out in the early 70s. I didn't know that word as a child. It was always referred to as 'up the garden', and it really was up! Up four steps and then a slope; a terrible route when frosty or after snow'. Snow could be just as much of a problem when it melted, as Mrs Hale of Coalpit Heath recalls. When the heavy snow of 1947 began to melt it all flowed in under the privy door; her mother stumbled up the path to the privy wearing her father's wellingtons, which were much too big. The present owner, Janet Drew, says that water still collects on the path outside the privy door in wet weather.

Walter Ford has some equally chilly memories. When the family moved to Redhill Farm, Elberton in 1949 the privy was still very much in use. It was a long walk down the garden to the 'Small House', which involved crossing a stream. The bridge was a single slab of stone with a wooden handrail, and this could get very slippery in damp weather. 'You had to be careful, especially in the dark. Mum slipped on the stone once, and I think I remember my sister Margaret falling into

Walter Ford standing outside the 'Small House' at Redhill Farm, Elberton. Converted to a WC in 1952, it remained the sole loo at the farm until 1970, when indoor facilities were installed.

the stream.' Margaret remembers the stream overflowing onto the path, so that she had to wear wellies for the journey to the privy with her younger brother Ashleigh. 'It was always me that had to go down with him with the lantern and lift him up onto the seat,' she said. Even if you had successfully negotiated the bridge, your troubles were not necessarily over. The flagstone floor used to rise up in frosty weather, so that it was very hard to get the door open. Once open it was impossible to close it again, and as the door faced north 'it used to be hellish draughty sat there with your trousers down and a north wind blowing!' Standing by the privy on a freezing January day made it easy to see what Walter meant!

In 1952 the house received mains water and electricity, and the first thing the family did was to convert the privy to a WC and install electric light. The old stone floor was replaced with concrete so that the door would now open and close easily, but having a WC brought other problems in harsh weather. To ensure that the water in the cistern didn't freeze, they used to bring down an infra-red light, normally used to keep the newborn calves warm. The old privy continued in regular use for many years, and in the 1960s Walter's father planted some conifers in front of the door to give it a little more privacy and to deflect the north wind. Eventually, in 1970, the family installed a WC in the farmhouse for Walter's father, who was ill and could no longer manage the walk. The 'Small House' is still used occasionally when anyone is working in the garden; the problem now is that it is not used often enough to stop the loo paper going damp!

[7]

THE PLEASANT RETREAT

While many people recall draughts, others' memories are of more comfortable privies. Ferry Cottages on the banks of the Avon at Warleigh, near Bath, has a pair of privies joined on to the back of the house. Dug into the bank of this sloping site, they are semi underground and sheltered from any draughts by both the house and the bank. Tony Parr remembers that it could be warmer out there than in the house, and he would go out to the privy to warm up! Set completely into the bank is a barrel-vaulted 'cellar' on the southern edge of Marshfield. According to the owner, Mr Hayes, this is supposed to have been a privy, although there is now no sign of its former use. It must have been relatively warm in there, especially on sunny days as it faces more or less due south.

I was often told of fathers or grandfathers going down to the privy for a quiet read or a smoke. Presumably they only lingered when the weather was warm enough. Keith Johnson of Bathford recalls that where he was brought up in Fairfield Park near Bath it was common for the menfolk to take the paper to the privy on a Sunday for an hour or so's quiet read. Kathleen Smith's grandfather did the same. 'There were other names for them [privies] I believe, but the only other I remember was when my Grampy was going up to use it, he would always say "I am going up to the House of Commons", and take the paper to read'. At Hall End Farm near Wickwar, Mary Hardwick's father used to take the newspaper and spend ages in there; she remembers them all (six children) queuing up outside waiting to use the loo. It was not only the

This vaulted cellar dug into the hillside in Marshfield is believed to have been a privy, although nothing remains now to show its former use.

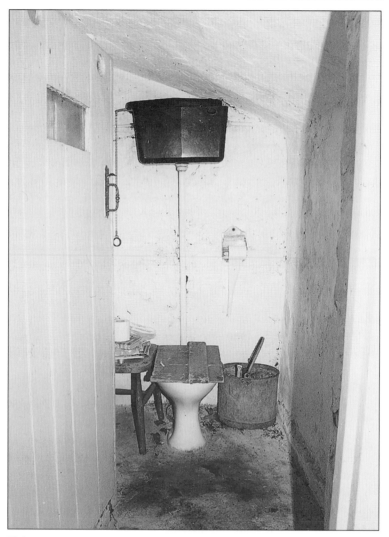

This snug privy built under the front terrace of a late 18th-century house in Wellsway, Keynsham is still in use, converted to a WC, a handy retreat for anyone who wants some peace and quiet!

adults who liked to sit in the privy and read. Mrs Cullimore remembers Railway Terrace at Rowley in Lower Cam, where a single privy served a row of four cottages! It was a three-holer, with the holes all different sizes, and was sited a long way from the house at the end of a large garden. She used to pick peas and fruit on her way to the privy, and eat them while reading her comic in privacy. Hopefully none of the other occupants of the cottages were kept waiting for too long! Sometimes the quiet read was disturbed, as Rodney Butcher recalls. 'Thinking back, I don't remember privies being fitted with bolts. Presumably the closed door was the only clue needed. This didn't always work, and I do remember a friend's sister being caught by the Council disposal crew at Wanswell reading the *Beano* with, of course, knickers decorating her ankles.' Just as people do now, others would escape to the loo to smoke. Mr Beard of Woodford told me that the children often saw smoke rising from next door's privy – their neighbour used to go out there for a quiet smoke of his pipe.

Other people just enjoyed the view. 'I recall visiting an elderly resident in this village, now deceased, not that many years ago,' wrote Marlene Gallop of Bitton, 'and not getting a reply from the doorknock went around to see if he was in his garden. He was sitting resplendently on his privy, door open. He apologised and said it was his fault but he never bothered to shut the door as he loved the view whilst sitting there.'

Sometimes the door was left open of necessity, as recalled by Mr Amos of Doynton. His privy has no window, so you had to take a torch; sometimes if it was not too cold, wet or windy you could leave the door open for light. This could be hazardous, as a public footpath runs along the side of the garden faced by the privy door. Two yew trees used to stand outside the door and hopefully would have been sufficient to shield users from the sight of anyone on the path! Other doors were too difficult to shut. Vera White wrote: 'During the winter months the door would stick with the damp so you couldn't shut it, not that you needed to, nobody could look in. Also if the moon was out it was better open.'

Privies are of course frequently surrounded by trees and foliage, sometimes to the extent that you cannot see the building at all! Fragrant plants such as honeysuckle and lilac are commonly found, and in the summer would add a pleasant fragrance. Fruit trees are equally likely to be next to the privy, and sometimes the falling fruit would make the occupant jump. Michael Clinch remembers his delight in such a tree at his grandparents' home in Olveston in the 1930s. 'Outside the loo on the right hand side was the most magnificent fig tree. Tall, wide and bountiful with large leaves and glorious green figs in summer, which used to delight me, with so many to pick that there was never any restriction for a young man with a sweet tooth.'

For a privy to be a pleasant enough location to spend time in, it had to be kept clean, the seat scrubbed and the walls limewashed. Cleaning was a job which usually fell to the women of the family. Marlene Gallop's grandparents lived in a Victorian terraced house in Bath. 'My mother (now 83) was born in that house and her recollections are of a wooden seat and surround which on washing day was scrubbed down by her using the old hot water left in the copper boiler after the washing was done.' Vera White has clear memories of her grandparents' privy at Tierley. 'It was situated down the back garden next to the wash house and Granny kept it spotless. The wooden seat and stone slab floor was scrubbed and a refreshing smell of Jeyes fluid made it more inviting.' The privy at Old Down Hill, Tockington, where Mary Hulbert's grandparents lived was a 'stone building semi-detached to the pigsty, and opposite the wooden chicken house. Hardly surprising that disinfectant powder was kept alongside the box of torn newspaper and used liberally'.

Limewashing often took place at the same time as the farm buildings were redone; Mrs Minchin used to scrub the seat and whitewash the walls of their privy in Yate along with the stable and pigsties. Maureen Moras's father 'used to lime-wash the walls [of the privy], usually at the same time as he was doing the back kitchens and the cowsheds. It was all nice and fresh when it was done'. Although white limewash was common, I have found evidence of many other colours surviving on privy walls. Yellow ochre, both a darker and a paler variety, seems to have been the most common, but I have also found pink, red, green and various shades of blue.

For personal hygiene, many people recall newspaper

The privy seat which decorates the garden wall in Marshfield where Jack Walters, a retired plumber, lives. The central recess would have held a box for the newspaper.

being hung on a nail for use as toilet paper. Kathleen Smith of Larkhall, Bath recalls their privy at Goosey. 'We had to cut up the newspaper in squares, poke a skewer to make a hole for the string and hang it on the door. (Thank goodness the print did not come off the paper like it does now.)' Other storage methods were sometimes used. The old privy seat which now adorns the garden wall of Jack Walter's home in Marshfield has a recess between the two holes for a small wooden box to hold the paper. June Broom told me that the newspaper cut into squares was kept in a pile on the side of the seat, and many privies have a small recess in the wall which could be used for this purpose.

Various newspapers were used; Vera White recalls that 'Our job was to cut the *Radio Times* pages into four which made the ideal size for use, then threaded on a string and hung on the nail.' Mary Knight of Marshfield remembers the *Farmers and Stockbreeders Weekly* being pressed into service, while her sister Christiana Poole told me that she used to enjoy reading the bits of newspaper but found it rather frustrating when she couldn't find the rest of the story! John Forster's grandparents lived in Berkeley, where 'toilet paper came in the form of whole copies of the *Berkeley Gazette*; you simply tore off what was needed'.

Whether it came in whole newspapers or neat squares, some people found that the newspaper needed some attention to make it usable. As Walter Ford recalls, nine-inch squares of newspaper were stacked on the windowsill and 'while you were sitting there you used to scrump the paper up in your hands to make it soft enough'. Later they graduated to Jeyes toilet paper in a packet. Patrick Bird also recalls the change to real toilet paper in a family privy: 'During the war years a pile of old newspapers passed for toilet paper there. My grandparents died round about 1960.

Any type of paper could be used in the loo – preferably soft and with something to read on it!

The author at Moorend Farm, Hambrook with newspapers dated 1986 (the last time it was used?) which were found in the 17th-century privy.

After that a dear spinster aunt (Auntie Daisy) did her best to keep it clean, often scrubbing the woodwork of the seats, and real toilet paper was made available.' Even in the 1930s, however, some people used real toilet paper; Michael Clinch remembers that 'the seat was not uncomfortable and within easy reach the wire toilet roll holder with its Bronco toilet roll – nothing downmarket about my mother'. Round the corner at his grandparents' house they were also very up-to-date. 'Here again was the ash bucket and roll of Bronco paper hanging on a string, and the musical white enamel slop bucket for "the roses".' 'Real' loo paper was certainly around well before the war, and my father told me that when he was in the army during the war, toilet paper was known as 'Army Form Blank'.

Before the advent of the soft loo roll, people used their ingenuity to provide something rather more pleasant than newspaper. Di Wilson of Almondsbury told me all about her grandparents' privy at Jasmine Cottage, Woodlands; it was a four-holer, all different sizes, built of stone with a tiled roof. 'It was immaculate, whitewashed inside, and Granfer scrubbed the wooden seat.' Di's other grandparents ran the shop on Almondsbury Hill from the 1920s onwards. Every morning they went down to the market by Temple Meads for fruit and ice cream from Covent Garden. Di used to smooth out the papers in which the South African oranges and grapefruit were wrapped, thread them on string using a huge bobbin needle, and take them along to Granny Meachin to use as a more comfortable alternative to newspaper. 'Oh, but they smelt lovely, those loos!' as the scent from the orange papers permeated the building. Orange papers were also used by Marlene Gallop's grandparents. 'The 'toilet paper' was old newspapers cut up. However, I remember being requested to bring back any fruit I purchased, when doing my grandmother's shopping, still in its tissue paper. This was about 48 years ago. I then had the task of unwrapping the fruit, smoothing out the tissue paper and threading it on to string. We were then able to have very colourful "luxury" toilet paper.' Maureen Moras told me that orange papers were regarded as very upmarket. Her Gran sometimes used glossy magazine paper, also 'upmarket but not very effective!'

[8]

MISHAPS AND MISCHIEF

Life with a privy produced some never-to-be-forgotten moments when mishaps occurred. In almost every instance, my correspondents told me of accidents which had happened to someone else; the person who would own up to being the victim themselves is rare indeed. However, when I visited Julian and Diana St John Brooks, who for many years ran the restaurant at The Manor House at Gaunts Earthcott, they were still able to laugh about Julian's mishap with a full privy bucket during their early married life. As Diana said, 'Julian had vivid memories of tripping (literally) with it en route to the vegetable patch, and I remember the excellent Brussels sprouts we grew!'

Julian was a retired army officer, but a bucket was also the downfall of a retired naval gentleman, as Chris Curtis of Olveston remembers. Mr James, a high-ranking officer in the Australian navy, retired to Alveston and lived next to the allotments. The entrance to the allotments was quite a way for an elderly gentleman to walk, so he decided to rig up a ladder over the garden wall. It was about six feet high, and was made of wood with the rungs made from lengths of iron pipe. 'To everyone on the allotment, this was a brilliant idea. Only Mr James could think of such an idea. Mr James would throw his tools into the allotment and then descend on the ladder to toil in the garden. All went well until one day the dreaded bucket covered with a sack appeared on the wall. Over came Mr James, stood on the ladder, and over came the bucket. Unfortunately, the bottom rim of the bucket caught in a topper [one of the upright stones on the top of a garden wall] and poor Mr James was covered all over from head to foot. The air was blue for a few minutes!' Chris recalled. 'For this deadly deed he earned himself a nickname from us boys; he was always known as "Jammy James".'

Chris also remembers that groups of children would meet outside the Cross Hands Inn at Alveston to play. One Sunday evening they played 'Chase the Foxes', when two children chosen to be foxes had to run off, leaving various clues as to which way they had gone. After a short while all the others would give chase. As Chris recalled, 'This could go on for miles, but what I'm going to tell was a very short trip!' One of his brothers (he had seven brothers and three sisters) and a cousin were chosen as the foxes, and after a short distance they decided to go through a patch of Brussels sprouts to throw the 'hounds' off their trail. 'These sprouts were known to be the best in the village, and everyone wondered why. My cousin soon found out the answer! He came out the other side smelling and looking rather messy, because this was where the contents of the dreaded bucket had been deposited!'

Clearly it took a long time before the filled trenches in the vegetable garden were safe to walk on. Someone else found this out the hard way, as Mr Browning of Thornbury wrote. 'My most amusing memory was at the farm where I worked. They had a double privy with a normal seat and a small one for children. One weekend the farmer's wife's brother, wife and children came to stay. They were very amused at the comic toilet facilities and the newspaper. On the Sunday morning Joe the husband came out in his suit trousers and new slippers. He decided he would walk between the black and red currant bushes and the raspberry canes. Before they came, the farmer had trenched between the rows and emptied and cleaned the privies. Before we could stop him he was right in the middle, and he had to walk right through to the end without his slippers. It covered half up his trousers. He never visited the farm again to my knowledge.' Hardly surprising that he didn't see the funny side, although the onlookers clearly did.

This victim was stone-cold sober, but too much to drink at the local pub caused Bill Hazell's downfall, as recalled by Norah Barnes. On his way home he fell into the cesspit of her uncle's privy; his clothes were out on the line for weeks to try and get rid of the smell! It must have been quite an incentive not to get drunk again, and I daresay his wife had a few choice words on the subject. The cesspit beside the privy at Ken and Eileen Prout's house in Chipping Sodbury claimed a younger victim, their nephew, who while playing in the garden caught his foot in the cesspit and fell in. 'He must have been about six at the time and he stank to high heaven!' said Eileen.

I imagine many things must have been lost down the hole too, but only one person has told me of such an incident. Marlene Gallop's mother 'remembers the loss of a precious chocolate doll given her as a Christmas gift which fell out of her pinnie and vanished down the toilet'. The poor child must have been mortified, and at the age of 83 clearly remembers the incident as if it were yesterday.

Two people recalled mishaps of a different nature, when unexpected visitors were found lurking in the privy. Dorothy Gay's sister Norah lived at Pound Farm, Almondsbury, where the single-holer was just outside the back door. One morning Norah had the fright of her life when she went out to use the privy and found an old tramp already installed on the seat. He had probably spent the night there to shelter from the cold, but she didn't stop to find out, but ran back into the house to recover herself!

Gladys Griffin of Clevedon remembers a similar incident.

'My Father tells me about the loo at Kenn where my mother lived. Their loo was built by the little road and she went out in the dark and sat on a tramp's lap. He was hoping to spend the night in the dry!' A well-built stone privy would of course have afforded a relatively comfortable night's shelter for a gentleman of the road, and if he timed it right he could remain undetected.

Some people seem to be accident-prone, but I could scarcely believe it when Mrs Beard of Woodford told me that she had been locked in a privy not once, but twice. The first occasion was in the early 1950s during a caravan holiday in South Wales. The site had a flush loo at the bottom of the field, but their small son was scared of this, as at home they still had an Elsan. He insisted that they take his potty with them to the loo, and as soon as he had finished he jumped up, ran out of the loo and pushed the door shut, leaving mum locked inside. He ran back up the field to the caravan, and although Mrs Beard called out for help, no one heard her. But she was a woman of some resource. In the end she used a hairgrip and picked the lock.

The second incident took place at their cottage in Damery Lane, where the small brick-built privy, now a coalshed, was used as a toolshed. One day Mrs Beard had gone to tidy it up when her three-year-old daughter Sandra pushed the door to and the latch clicked shut. Unable to open the door from the inside, she realised that her daughter was probably too short to reach the latch. She therefore asked Sandra to get a stick and push the latch up, but she either didn't understand or couldn't manage this task. Mrs Beard was panicking, worried that Sandra might get out onto the road. 'I remember it was a Friday because the grocer came round about 4 o'clock, as they did in those days, and I wondered if I'd have to wait until then to be let out. It must have been about half past two at

Mr and Mrs Beard outside their privy in Woodford, where their toddler daughter locked Mrs Beard in. The door in which she cut a hole to escape has been replaced.

the time.' Eventually she managed to find a small saw among all the tools in the shed and cut a hole in the top of the door big enough to get her hand out. 'I must have used a piece of wire or something, and managed to open the latch.' Since then the door has been replaced, so the escape hole is no longer to be seen. After these experiences, she could have had a future as an escape artist!

There have been no suggestions of haunted privies but an early-morning visit to a privy may have led one man to believe that he had seen a ghost. Dick Knight of Castle Farm at Marshfield told me the story. The privy is set against the wall not far from the road, which is lower than the garden. Early one morning, when it was still dark, a young postman was coming along the lane when he saw a head looking over the garden wall. Believing he had seen a ghost he fled in terror and never again delivered letters there in the dark. The family suggested that what he may in fact have seen was Dick's great grandfather, who was living there at the time, heading for the privy in his white nightshirt. Whatever it was, it had a dramatic effect on him. Forty or more years later, the former postman was working at the farm. When he was in the kitchen having his coffee break, Dick casually asked him to tell the ghost story to the children, thinking to amuse them. 'He went as white as a sheet. He never said a word. He was all of a tremble. It was so embarrassing – I wished I'd never asked.'

Some unfortunate happenings were not accidents at all, but the result of deliberate pranks perpetrated almost invariably by the male of the species – Political Correctness has no place in the history of the privy. Some were harmless

fun, others a little more vindictive. Reg Poole remembers
sitting on a privy at his cousins' house in Gloucester, when his
cousin quietly opened the door at the back and tickled his
bottom with a brush, making him jump. Stinging nettles were
used in Littleton, and the perpetrators felt that the results were
worth the punishment they subsequently received. Maureen
Moras's maternal grandfather told of a time when some boys at
Littleton School waited until the lady teacher was in the privy
before opening the door and pushing some stinging nettles
through. Nothing at all was said about the incident, but all the
boys were severely caned – they all knew why!

In Acton Turville Miss Freda Brown remembers her father
Arthur playing lots of tricks on them when they were in the
privy. Once when her cousin Joan was ensconced within,
Arthur crept up the neighbour's path and lobbed a tray over
the fence in front of the privy door. Poor Joan ran down the

A tempting pair of trapdoors – surely conducive to mischief!

path, frightened to death by the sudden noise, and with her knickers in her hand. Husbands also liked trying to frighten their wives. Janet Drew of North Road, Yate told me that if her husband knew she was in the privy, he used to creep down the path and shower small stones onto the roof to make her jump!

Chris Curtis of Olveston has some similar stories of his boyhood in Alveston in the 1940s. One of eleven children, he remembers a near neighbour who was 'rather stout and rather old and sometimes rather miserable if we went to retrieve our ball from her garden'. With such a large family, this must have happened quite frequently. Her privy backed on to a small back lane, where there was a trapdoor for the removal of the bucket. This gave Chris and his co-conspirators their chance. 'We would watch for her going to the privy late at night carrying her candle, her only means of light. We would wait a few minutes, then the flap would be removed and a hail of stones would be thrown at the bucket. The poor lady must have been terrified.'

Almost next door lived a good friend of the children's father, 'but this made no difference to us children!' His privy had a corrugated iron roof, which 'as far as we were concerned, was a sitting duck target.' said Chris. The victim of their mischief here was the son of the house, who would settle himself in there for a long session. To keep himself entertained 'he would often be heard giving a commentary on his favourite football team, which happened to be Bristol City. At the climax of this commentary when a goal was scored, it was not a volume of applause he would hear, but about ten handfuls of gravel or any other objects to hand'. This must have made a devastating noise on the tin roof, and as Chris said, 'My word, how scary'. The poor boy must have jumped out of his skin!

The long gardens belonging to the row of three cottages in Acton Turville where Miss Freda Brown remembers riding her bike to the privy, and where her father played a trick on her cousin. The roof of the privy next door can just be seen above the wall on the left.

[9]

CHILDHOOD MEMORIES

People's memories of how they felt about privies as children
vary enormously. Michael Clinch recalls a 'not unpleasant
musty smell about the place, with its earth floor and just a
touch of dampness'. Many children, however, seem to have
disliked using the old privy, finding it dark, cold, smelly or
frightening. Patrick Bird 'used to hate going there as a child.
It was a smelly and dark place, often festooned with cobwebs
in which large spiders lurked'. Nellie Garland has similar
unpleasant memories. 'We spent each summer holiday at
West Horrington near Wells, where my mother was born.
Coming from all mod cons to Gran's house was quite a
culture shock, and I remember the privy at the back of the
house – how I hated that place, the old stone walls seemed
alive with mice, spiders, beetles and all sorts of creepy
things.' Pauline Preddy used to hate her aunt's privy – there
were gaps at the top and bottom of the door and it smelt!

The banter of older brothers and sisters did not help, as
Sarah Spratt of Alveston recalls. 'I am the youngest of our
family of eight, so my brothers delighted in teasing me about
the "bogey man" in the cabbages which made the journey
"up the garden" quite a challenge.' Wartime too could make
venturing outside to the privy quite an ordeal for a small
child. Marlene Gallop's mother 'remembers being too
frightened to go outside during the bombing and just "held
out",' while Christiana Poole recalls being told to be very
careful when using a torch during the blackout.

David Hart had a rather different sort of frightening

Churchill House, Olveston has the lift-out type of trapdoor in the front of the seat, safe from pranksters!

experience. He lived at 4 Wilson Terrace in the St Paul's area of Bristol, while his gran lived three doors along at number one. It was a large terraced house and in the area at the back of the houses, underneath a terrace, were the toilets, originally privies but converted to flush toilets with wooden seats. Gran, however, did not modernise her habits; on one occasion David, then a small boy, went to use her loo after she had been in. He ran out quickly; 'Quick Gran, the lavatory's on fire!' 'Don't worry about that; I do that to kill the smell!' she laughed. 'I had such a shock when I went in there after she had used it because there were still flames in the pan – she used to put a piece of newspaper down the pan and light it. It frightened me to death the first time I saw it.'

For some children the problem was a one-holer with its adult-sized hole rather than the two or even three-holers which had one hole specially designed for small behinds! However, no one remembered anyone falling in. Vera White recalled that 'the visits to the privy were quite eventful at times, even sitting on the seat was quite scary – it seemed such a vast hole for a little bottom. Visiting the "loo" during the day was alright but after dark it was a challenge to children, a quick dash if raining hard guided by light from the old bicycle lamp, then a quick dash back especially if owls were hooting'. Maureen Moras 'used to drum my heels on the front of the seat, which was made of wood. It had a single hole and I remember rocking a bit on the large hole'.

Other children had different reasons to dislike the privy. In his *Almondsbury Memories*, Frank Gastrell wrote of the medicines that were administered to keep them 'regular'. 'After all the high living over Christmas – which only a few were used to – stomach upsets were to be expected. The children were given an extra dose of liquorice powder and the older ones had Epsom Salts. This meant several journeys to that little house at the bottom of the garden, called by some the privy, and by others the Houses of Parliament, because so many sittings took place there. The liquorice powder or senna tea was given to the youngsters on Saturday night. Sometimes they were given with an ulterior motive; the youngsters liked to vanish soon after breakfast on a Sunday morning and only re-appear for dinner, thinking to avoid going to Sunday School. For obvious reasons the doses kept them near the house.'

While some children submitted to the inevitable and used the dreaded privy, others found ways of avoiding it. In *A Bristol Child* Nina Rollason writes: 'The earth closet was at the very top of the garden and was so smelly that we preferred to squat in the long grass instead of using it.' Norah Barnes used the loo at home before visiting her grandparents so as not to have to use the privy; 'It was horrible down there,' she recalled. The move to a property with an outside privy could be a devastating experience, for a teenager used to indoor facilities. In 1932 Dorothy Gay's father moved the family from a house with all mod cons to the White Lion at Yate where the only facility was a two-seater privy also used by the customers. Poor Dorothy found the whole set-up horrific, and one of the first things her mother did was to turn one of the bedrooms into a proper bathroom. Dorothy remembers her cousin's house at Avebury in Wiltshire, which had a three-seater. 'I couldn't bear to go in there,' she said. 'They used to smell awful. I used potties instead, but I also made friends with the daughter at the Red Lion so that I could go and use their proper loo!'

Not all pubs had a proper loo, however. Mrs Cavin of Tockington recalls a visit to a country pub which had a two-seater privy, much to the amusement of her mum and her aunt, who roared with laughter. She herself was horrified and refused to use it.

Some children had their first experience of outside privies when they were evacuated from Bristol and Bath to the countryside during the Blitz. Keith Johnson recalled that they spent the first night of the Bath Blitz in bed, the second night under the stairs, and on the third night they left. People were streaming out of Bath, terrified by Lord Haw-Haw's promise that the city would be flattened, with their goods piled on prams and handcarts. The children were sent to stay with their father's brother who farmed at Cross Hands near Chipping Sodbury. He and his brother spent the mornings in school and the afternoons helping on the farm with the two girls who lived there. He remembers a four-holer privy in a shed in the corner of a field, set over an underground stream which he believes was 100 feet down. The children used to go to the privy all together and have a competition to see whose offerings would hit the water first!

The novelty element was clearly at work here, and town children visiting their country cousins often found the privy rather fun. June Broom told me that 'when relatives from Cardiff used to visit, the children used to like going up to the privy with the lantern, which they placed on the windowsill; this was a great novelty, as at home they had indoor plumbing'. Beryl Penny has a similar story, but in this instance she was the visitor, coming from Cardiff to visit relatives in a cottage in Easter Compton. It had a two-seater, same-level privy close to the house, and when the family came over on a visit, she used to think it great fun to use the old-fashioned facilities.

Another privy with happy memories is still very much intact at Furzedown Farm, Tockington. When Mr and Mrs Pearce came in 1966 there was no mains water, only a pump outside the back door. They immediately installed a WC in the spacious brick-built privy, leaving the old wooden seats

The substantial brick privy at Furzedown Farm, Tockington is on the left; the former stone lean-to privy can be seen in the corner, close to the back door.

The seats survive intact in the brick privy, complete with their lids with finger holes and the panelled back. The compartment on the left was for ashes. This is the scene of Mary Hallett's musings.

intact. On one occasion they were visited by Mrs Mary Hallett, who taught their daughter Mollie at Olveston School. She went out to use the loo in the privy, and when she failed to reappear they began to get anxious about her. When Mrs Pearce went to see what had happened, she found her sitting out there reminiscing about the holidays she spent there as a child. Obviously the old privy with its double seat and compartment for ashes held happy memories for her and she was delighted to find it still intact. The brick privy must have been built in Victorian times, or possibly even later, and replaced an old stone lean-to privy built against the wall near the kitchen door.

Mary Hulbert lived on Old Down Hill, where 'I remember school friends thinking it was fun to have to "go up the garden", and smaller children insisting on the need to do so as soon as they arrived. By my twenties I was rather self-conscious about inviting friends home because of the set-up, though by then we had progressed through tissue paper to toilet rolls. However, I can't remember anyone I brought home being embarrassed or ill at ease – if they were they didn't show it'.

[10]

THE PRIVY TODAY

As readers will have gathered, the privy, or at any rate the privy building, is alive and well in south Gloucestershire in vast numbers. The survival rate can be attributed to two things. Firstly, the buildings are very solidly constructed of local stone or brick, and secondly, the late arrival of mains sewers in many villages meant that the privies were often still in use until the late 1960s. This was certainly the case in Olveston and Tockington, where I have seen fifteen privies. Some have been in use more recently still, as old habits die hard. I was told that when piped water and mains drainage came to Kelston in about 1946 or 1947, one lady refused to have such a disgusting thing as a water closet inside her house!

Presumably the 17th-century inhabitants of Kelston felt the same, as Sir John Harington's invention did not instantly become the latest 'must-have' feature. The lady concerned clearly thought it far more hygienic to go 'down the garden', and I must admit to a sneaking sympathy with her point of view. Wallace Reyburn, writing in *Flushed With Pride: The Story of Thomas Crapper*, points out two snags to the modern WC One is that scientists discovered that 'flushing a wash-down water closet produces a bacterial aerosol' and that the effect is worse if it is flushed with the lid closed. The second is that 'since plastic bolted to glazed pottery never has been or ever will be as secure as a metal bolt in wood, the modern plastic toilet seat in no time starts to drift off its moorings'. Having struggled to refix our loo seat with the very inadequate plastic bolts, I feel that there is a lot to be said for the securely fixed plank with a simple hole in the centre!

Some privies have not stood the test of time, and have for various reasons been demolished. The picturesque ruins of the privy at Morton Maypole near Thornbury have now gone, despite its original 18th-century door with a typical doorhandle of that period. In Almondsbury, one ruined privy has recently been demolished, while another survives (just) at the end of a garden in Over Lane. The present owners have lived in the house for over fifty years, but never knew the privy to have had a door. Instead there was a wooden screen in front of the doorway, and the emptying hole was reached through the henhouse at the side. I was too late to see the lean-to privy behind a house in Chipping Sodbury High Street, as the rear of the house had been renovated a few months previously. Graham Elliott, the owner, had found the remains of a double seat and, inside

Only the seat survives, alongside the ruined privy on the back of the bakehouse at Rock House, Elberton.

the house, a cistern under the kitchen floor, which collected
all the rainwater from the roof. This was then channelled
through the privy to a soakaway pit in the garden. Others
were demolished a long time ago. Mrs Meredith told me that
they had had a 'two hole, same level' privy at Village Farm in
Elberton, but that they demolished it as it was 'rather
dilapidated'. At Chestnut Farm at Mayshill the remains of the
vault privy were turned into a sandpit for the children, while
Barbara Adams of Charfield has remodelled the old privy
and pigsty as her toolshed.

Others have been reincarnated as henhouses, woodsheds,
coalsheds and toolsheds. It seems that the average privy is
just the right size for the lawnmower; tools can be propped
neatly against the walls or hung from racks, and shelves can
be installed for plant pots and other gardening
paraphernalia. Trevor Anderson also has an Elsan in his
privy-cum-toolshed in Olveston, which can be very handy if
you need the loo while gardening and do not wish (or are
not allowed) to trail through the house in muddy boots! I
found about a dozen which have had WCs installed, some of
which are still in use. At Rose Cottage in Tockington the WC
has now gone, but it was put in by the previous owner who,
although disabled, loved gardening. It saved her from having
to struggle upstairs to the indoor loo.

While many of these privies have simply been kept in good
repair, others have been restored from a ruinous condition.
The privy at Olveston Court is a good example, and now not
only functions as a very useful shed but also bears a delightful
weather vane. (The 17th-century one at Hall End Farm
carries the television satellite dish, a wonderful juxtaposition
of old and new.) A splendid job of restoration has been
carried out at Patch Farm, near the Gloucester-Sharpness
canal at Slimbridge. The owner, Martin Brown, and his

Barbara Bennett holds the double seats outside the family privy at Sayscourt Farm; she and her husband hope to restore it. Note the curved wall next to the entrance.

Restoration nearing completion at Patch Farm, Slimbridge; owner Martin Brown watches while Ken White perches on the ladder.

The privy and the house at Patch farm were both built around 1780, and it's a fair walk down the garden, especially in the dark!

friend Ken White have spent their Saturdays for the past two years restoring it, and are justifiably proud of the result. The privy at Patch Farm, although small, has some of the best architectural details I have seen. The brick walls have round-headed blank arches on each side, with keystones which match those over the windows of the house, and both have stone-tiled roofs. There can be little doubt that the privy was built at the same time as the house in about 1780. The floor has red sandstone flags, shipped across the river from the Forest of Dean. The privy roof had to be replaced, as did the door and the seat, and the restoration has used exactly the same materials as the original – oak for the beaded doorframe, elm for the door, the seat and the rafters. The timbers for the restoration came from a demolished decoyman's cottage at the Wildfowl Trust, where Martin

90

works. The privy is built over a ditch which fills up with water in wet weather, and when they dug out the channel they found fresh ashes and a tube of pile ointment! The old gentleman who lived there, Mr John Workman, was certainly using it until 1963, although Ken believes that his father may have been the last person to use it when he was doing some work for the subsequent owner in 1968.

The restoration at Patch Farm is now complete and another important piece of our heritage has been saved for future generations to wonder at. Elsewhere, the work is still to be completed. At both Sayscourt Farm, Mayshill and Luces Farm, Rockhampton necessary work has been carried out to the roof and the walls, but the seats have yet to be reinstated. These buildings are all being restored out of interest in the

Rodney Butcher's privy at Newport has two unusual arched recesses, whose shape suggests that it was built in the late 18th century for the old cottage which used to stand on the site. The seat is still in place, albeit rather rickety, and a bird has built its nest in the recess behind.

past, but will anyone, I wonder, be brave enough to restore one to everyday use? Perhaps Rodney Butcher is the man to do it. He writes, 'The property at Newport, where I was born and raised, is interesting in itself, being constructed from two "retired" railway carriages, in the early 30s, laid side by side and with a roof built over the top. The carriages date from around 1875. Together with three sisters I lived there without the benefit of electricity, with water pumped from a well outside, and, of course, using what we called a "bucket lavatory". It was hidden behind a large shrub, bearing, in the season, heavily scented flowers. The bucket was emptied by my father into trenches dug in the garden. Our constant supply of excellent fresh fruit and vegetables must have represented a fairly direct form of recycling! We left the property around 1966 but it still stands in good condition. The privy is not in such good condition. Its roof has fallen in, the walls are unstable and it is surrounded by brambles. However, as I propose renovating the whole, for holiday lets, I do intend digging it out and rebuilding in its original form.' It would be a novel selling-point for a holiday cottage to have a functioning privy, but I doubt that is quite what he has in mind. Still, you never know!

ACKNOWLEDGEMENTS

I would like to record my thanks to the many people who have made this book possible, both the owners of privies and all the other people who have provided information. I even gleaned useful snippets of information while at the dentist and the hairdresser! I am grateful to the editors of the *Thornbury and Dursley Gazette*, the *Western Daily Press*, the *Bath Chronicle*, and many parish magazines and newsletters for publishing my appeals for information. Their readers responded marvellously. Thanks are due particularly to Tony Crouch, who generously put all his researches on plumbing in Bath at my disposal; without his contribution I would have had little to write on the subject. Thank you too to John Bryant and Dr Roger Leech for information and illustrations on Bristol loos; to Mary Isaac of Hall End Farm, Wickwar, Peris Jones of the Downend History Group, and Jack Walters of Marshfield, who have all been so helpful in providing me with useful contacts; to Michael Clinch for allowing me to use the relevant sections of his as yet unfinished auto-biography (I hope he manages to finish it); to everyone who has written or telephoned with tales to tell and to all the owners of privies who have received me into their homes, gardens and farmyards, told me stories and plied me with most welcome cups of tea and coffee. I am only sorry that at the end of the day I wasn't able to use everyone's contri-bution so to those whose story or privy has not been included in these pages, my very sincere apologies.

Thanks are also due especially to my long-suffering family. My parents, Fred and Betty Cook, were left to field many of the telephone calls; they wrote down innumerable messages for me, and my mum gallantly asked all her friends and acquaintances if they had a privy or a story to tell. My husband Mike is unfailingly supportive of my research activities, no matter how eccentric, and accompanied me on some of my privy visits. My elder daughter Catherine proved herself a most useful assistant and entertaining companion, but my younger daughter Elizabeth found privies cold, damp, draughty and boring and wanted nothing whatever to do with them!

This row of five privies at Creephole House, Didmarton was built within living memory, replacing earlier ones in a lean-to attached to the cottages. (Photo courtesy of Anne Walsh)

ODE TO THE GARDEN PRIVY

Privies of South Gloucestershire, the subject of this book,
Where many an ancient farmstead is worth a second look
To see if in one corner beside the lilac sweet
Is a little stone-built privy with a double wooden seat.

And some are next to pigsties and some the garden wall,
While other ones have tumbled down with nothing left at all.
And some are maintained lovingly to serve as garden sheds,
The woodhouse or the coalhouse among the flower beds.

And some had buckets, some had pits, and had some
    running water,
And everybody's vegetables grew better than they oughta.
The dreadful modern hygiene rules would ban this ancient
    system,
But ecologically it's sound and better than a cistern

This aspect of our history has rarely been recorded;
To the mind of modern humans it's regarded as quite sordid.
Yet these splendid little buildings are a valuable part
Of everybody's past and of the privy-builder's art.

So let's record these monuments of England's social history,
Save memories, take photographs and celebrate THE PRIVY.